Until Death Do Us Part, But Before That

By Barbara Bailey

A Short Story and Tips for Middle-America Spouses

Before Becoming a Widow or Widower

Cover art by the Author "Oceanview"

INSIDE

Barbara Bailey authored a short story "Unpleasant Business" after the passing of her husband. She wanted to share tips for easing frustrations and obstacles for transitioning to life as a widow or widower. She noted that while the upper class typically is well funded and plans well in advance, and underserved people are supported with government and charity resources, but today's American middle-class senior women in particular faced unique challenges. She shares personal accounts of her transition, suggestions for preparation in advance for couples, and a useful checklist of critical data and details to share with your partner before the inevitable … until death do us part.

ABOUT THE AUTHOR

Barbara Bailey was born in Manhattan, graduated cum laude from Mount St. Mary's College in New York, and operated a successful Bed and Breakfast in the Hudson Valley. She and her husband moved to Palm Beach County to retire. In South Florida, Barbara is an artist, art teacher and active in the art community.

Title:
Until Death Do Us Part,
But Before That

Published in the USA

Written by:
Barbara Bailey

International Standard Book Number
ISBN number 979-8-218-02546-5

CONTENTS

Preface

Chapters

Family File Notes pages for your personal notes

PREFACE

Dear Reader,

Death! No one other than the Funeral Director wants to think about it. However, no matter how we ignore it, the inevitable will occur.

This book has been written in response to the many surprises that I and others personally experienced at the time of losing a loved one. I am hoping to prevent this "unpleasant business" from occurring while others are navigating this sad journey.

I begin this book with a short story that is based on a brief encounter. I call it "Unpleasant Business." In the story, the protagonist believes that she has made the appropriate preparations by having a will in place, etc. However, she is in for a few surprises.

"The loss that leads to despair, is the loss of our own sense of confidence in our future." --anonymous

CHAPTER 1,
Unpleasant Business, A Short Story

"You're kidding, I don't believe this, how can this be? I had a one o'clock appointment! This is the third time I have asked you what is going on," 75-year-old Veronica Blake addressed the woman behind the Social Security receptionist's desk.

The woman, thin lipped, officious, with a sallow complexion and an unfortunate face viewed her like a loathe-some insect.

"We're short staffed today Ma'am," She replied, "Just take a seat in the waiting area and Mr. Valentine will see you when he's free."

"I have had a seat for an hour and a half and I would like to remind you that I had an appointment which, by the way, took three weeks to get. Is there no one else I can see?" asked Veronica.

The receptionist glared over her steel rimmed glasses at the tall attractive woman.

"No," she sniffed, "Afraid not. Have a seat ma'am, probably won't be much longer."

Veronica turned on her Brooks Brothers heels and clicked across the highly glossed floor to the waiting area where a crowd of people sat. The scent of Chanel No. 5 wafting from her in the chilled office air. She sat and examined her beautifully French manicured nails reflecting the fluorescence from above and swallowed her frustration.

For the next half hour, Veronica sat imperiously and sulked. It had been two hours. She was not used to being treated like an object, a number, another irritant in someone's day. Her husband Ronald had always sheltered and protected her from all unpleasant business. Now, since his death, she was navigating in uncharted waters. Confused and intimidated by uncaring bureaucrats and insipid lackeys. Now it was incessant trips to the courthouse; waiting in line, the Social Security Office, waiting in line ... Attorney's offices, financial advisor's offices, banks and insurance companies. Hours on end on the phone, she spent waiting, taking up all her precious time. She had even had to give up her bridge game!

"How does one endure these constant assaults on one's psyche?" she thought.

Veronica ran her hands through her magnificently cut and marmalade colored hair. "Ronald," she thought. "How am I to live without you? What am I to do without you?"

Tears began to well up and threatened to ruin her perfectly applied makeup. She felt it was inappropriate to weep in public, but lately it happened unexpectedly. She would suddenly burst into tears at the most inopportune times. As she searched in her Louis Vuitton Purse for a handkerchief, tears slid down her handsome, patrician face.

She rose quickly and headed to the ladies' room to have another unexpected cry.

"Here now, what's this all about? Why the tears?" a soft caring voice asked.

Veronica looked up to see a concerned and kindly woman, about 60-years-old, wearing a polka-dot dress that covered her ample frame. She had on horn rimmed glasses and was holding a clutch of papers.

"Tell me what's wrong," she soothed, "First, what's your name?"

Veronica, upon hearing the compassion of the woman's voice began to cry more.

2

"Ver...on...ica," she answered, sobbing into her handkerchief.

"I'm Tamisha. What's so terrible that you're here crying in the ladies' room, Dear?" she asked.

"My husband died recently," Veronica answered.

"I'm so lost and lonely. I don't seem to be able to function and my life is shattered and I don't know what to do." She sobbed, "I can't sleep at night and when I do, I wake up in a panic. No one understands. And I break out into tears whenever I think of Ronald because I always went to him and he would know what to do. Oh, I am so sorry to tell you all of this."

"Well Dear," Tamisha said, as she adjusted her glasses, "I do understand because I lost my husband four years ago and what you're going through and the way you're feeling sounds very normal to me, so there's no need to apologize. I went through it and the loss isn't any less painful today, but it is different. You learn to cope. Tell me, what are you here for today?"

"I am filing for my husband's Social Security because mine is considerably less than his. I had to wait three weeks before I got an appointment. Meanwhile, last month's Social Security money was removed from the account by the bank and I had no idea. With his death the pension ended. The bank put a freeze on the joint account without ever notifying me and I didn't find out until a check bounced. Fortunately, I had savings in a different bank account and I used that to pay the recurring monthly payments on his credit cards. That really could have cost me a lot of money in bounced checks. So now here I am. I have waited two hours with an appointment and I am still waiting." she whined.

"Tell you what Veronica, I have some time now, so why don't we go to my computer and fill out the necessary forms? I can forward them to Mr. Valentine and they will be all ready to go by the time you are called. Dry your tears, follow me and let's get started," suggested Tamisha.

Veronica completed the forms with Tamisha, thanked her and returned to the waiting area where she sat next to an elderly woman wearing a faded blue dress and sneakers. Her limp gray hair was plaited into a single braid behind her back and she wore no make-up.

"This certainly is a busy place," Veronica said to the woman.

"Yes," the woman replied, "This is the third time I have had to come here."

"Really? If you don't mind my asking, why three times?" asked Veronica.

"Bureaucratic processes," she retorted. "I am attempting to get an increase to my deceased husband's Social Security payment."

"Oh," Veronica replied, "you lost your husband too?"

"Three years ago, and not only did I lose my husband, but I lost everything else too."

"What do you mean? What happened?" asked the alarmed Veronica.

"Well, you'll probably find out for yourself if all you have to live on is Social Security," the woman continued, "My husband Dan was an auto mechanic. He made a decent living. We had a nice home and a car; it was a reasonable middle- class life and we were content. He was a kind and decent man. It was devastating when he was diagnosed with pancreatic cancer. He was gone in three months."

She paused, took a breath and continued, "He had a small insurance policy which covered most of the

4

funeral expenses and some of the medical bills. I never had a career. I stayed home when the children were young and baby-sat or cleaned houses for a few extra dollars. When the kids got bigger, I sold beauty products. We had a savings account which I used to pay the recent bills because it took three months for the Social Security check awarded to me to finally arrive. Meanwhile I had to live and pay the bills. I have no other income and who's going to hire a 70-year-old woman? By the way, my name is Norma, what's yours?"

"I am Veronica. What about your children?" Veronica inquired, "Couldn't they help?"

The woman studied her hands and went on, "I had two children, a boy and a girl. My son was killed in April of 1965 during the U.S. invasion of the Dominican Republic. My daughter got married several years ago and moved to San Diego and her husband's mother moved in with them when her husband died so there was nowhere for me to go. You'd be surprised at how quickly the money disappears. I had to sell my home and I moved into a one-bedroom apartment. I pay the rent out of the proceeds from the sale of my home. Social Security pays me $900 a month. I babysit three days a week so I have money for food and medicine. I'm not alone in this situation; many other widows live in my humble community, too. Did you know that statistics say that a widow will live at least 14 years after her spouse dies? Also, an American widow will see a 37% decrease in income. The median income for women over the age of 65 is $17,000 per year. My husband worked hard all his life and although I only worked part time outside our home, I did what I could. We lived a law abiding, honorable life. I never thought it would be like this. I gave a son for this country, and although I have a caring daughter she is far away and can do nothing for me. I even thought about suicide but I'm a Catholic. Now, aren't you sorry you asked?"

Veronica was stunned by Norma's candor. She began to recognize the significance of her own situation.

"I never thought about what would happen," she said. "I guess I just never thought things through. I know we made a will and appointed designated beneficiaries on our bank accounts, but it is so much more complicated than that. I lost my husband Ronald's pension when he died, so the only income I will have is what Social Security will award me. I doubt at my age that I could find a decent paying job. I paid off all the funeral, medical and credit card bills with the insurance money and I am living on what's left from that policy but by next year it will be almost gone. I had only one son and we are estranged. We haven't spoken in ten years and I doubt he would be of any help."

"Welcome to the club!" Norma said bitterly.

With that, the clerk called for Norma Racine to see Mr. Valentine.

She said, as she parted, "Good Luck! You're gonna' need it!"

She disappeared into the cubicle.

"So," thought Veronica, her tenuous future stretched before her. A great empty maw spread across a wasteland of the slow, silent creeping of impoverishment. For without significant financial means, in very little time she would become part of those horrifying statistics. Icy streamers of fear feathered along her spine. "Oh my God, what will I do?" she thought. The loneliness, the emptiness and the grief combined with being impoverished washed over her in a frigid wave. It was like a click of the kaleidoscope and in one miniscule turn, in that crackling instant, her world shattered.

From the sweet safety and security of comfort; without warning, she is snatched and hurled into the cruel wall of adversity. She envisioned herself being homeless. A fog of depression settled over her mind and soul. She has been abandoned. The wonderful human being who loved and protected her; the one she depended upon, no longer exists and without him, her future is secured in loss and deprivation. Like Norma Racine, she would descend into a cold bitterness and callous discontent, as a woman dissolute and bereft.

All at once a great commotion began. She heard Norma's pleading voice and it seemed like an argument ensued. There was a silence, then suddenly Mr. Valentine was calling for help. Veronica rushed towards the cubicle and saw that Norma had collapsed. Veronica was shocked and frozen in place. Suddenly Tamisha rushed in and placed a bundled-up sweater beneath Norma's head. An ambulance was called.

Tamisha looked accusingly at Mr. Valentine and asked, "What happened?"

Sheepishly, he said, "We were discussing why her social security payment could not be increased … she became agitated and collapsed."

"It's quite sad," Tamisha said to Veronica, who stood saucer eyed beside her, "That woman has untreated high blood pressure which can lead to a stroke. Passing out here may have saved her life. If she can't afford medical treatment, it's only a matter of time."

The EMTs arrived, took over, placed Norma on a gurney and wheeled her to the waiting ambulance.

"Oh my God! This cannot be my fate as well. Think! Think! Veronica. Don't panic! Think! You still have time to make a plan. What to do?" Veronica thought as desperation crawled along the back of her brain.

"But wait, wait! I have an idea. What about Charles? Of course, there's Charles who was Ronald's best friend. He is a widower and is quite financially secure. Yes, yes, that's it – Charles!" Veronica smiled at this revelation.

Charles had always found her attractive. Nothing was ever overtly implied but a woman knows when a man is interested.

Veronica thought, "Oh, thank Heavens! Norma's fate is not my fate … I will not allow it! I will be relentless in my pursuit of Charles and he will be my savior. No, I won't let poverty and despair be my future. I will be adored and petted and spoiled again. I am a beautiful, loving and intelligent woman whose future will be as I choose it to be. I will not accept despair! I will not accept despair!"

"Veronica Blake to cubicle four," a woman's voice echoed in the cold harsh light, "Mr. Valentine will see you now."

The Short Story and Past Societal Mores

An interesting thing occurred when a younger male friend read the short story.

He asked, "Why doesn't Veronica just get a job?"

My character Veronica was depicted as a spoiled self-centered child-like woman who found herself in a situation where she had to face the problem of a reversal of fortune. However, the circumstances that she found herself in, were not of her own doing. The societal mores of the past helped lead her to her dilemma!

The Short Story and "Biology as Destiny"

In the 1940s, 1950s and into the 1960s there were very limited choices for women in the U.S. Women did not have access to birth control then as do women of today. Abortion was illegal and it was a disgrace to oneself and one's family to become pregnant out of wedlock. If that happened, many women committed suicide or had back-alley abortions. Women did not get hired for high paying jobs simply because employers assumed that any women of child bearing age would become pregnant and leave.

Women who worked in the factories during the war were let go and the soldiers returning replaced them. Women were discouraged from working outside the home. Society dictated that they stay at home and care for the extended family. The husband was the breadwinner. A woman went to college to find a husband, not necessarily to prepare for a job. Many women who didn't marry became secretaries, nurses or teachers, however the stigma of pregnancy still limited their options. I recall going to work at 16-years-old for the telephone company. I was subjected to a gynecological exam prior to hiring me as a condition of hiring … to make certain I showed no signs of pregnancy. Also, working women were constantly sexually harassed. There was no Me-Too movement or protection from predatory employers. It was safer to stay home.

As a result, now we have many middle-class older women who have no employable skills, and are left without a husband and with very few resources. Not many 75 or 80-year-old women can compete in today's market or are physically capable of holding a stressful job. It is not their fault that circumstances beyond their control left them in a stressful situation!

9

They, through no fault of their own, were coerced into being financially cared for by men. Many restrictions were imposed on us women. For example, at one time women could not have credit cards in their own name. The modern woman has now become financially secure by being able to compete in the job market and be financially independent.

CHAPTER 2,
Clear the Smoke,
A Note from the Short Story Author

People don't have to be as lost as the character Veronica in the "Unpleasant Business" short story. Dealing with institutional entities that are not known for compassion, can be frustrating and discouraging. Many widows are lost and overwhelmed with details of managing finances and daily living arrangements. The key to overcoming many frustrations is to have candid, frank conversations between spouses before either spouse or significant other passes. Then be prepared. Make a comprehensive family file of all details of how to run the household when either of the individuals pass. To be effective, each needs to share all the pertinent information. This also applies to those who are sharing the household and their lives together.

I had a list that my husband put together, but it was incomplete. For example, how was I to know that Smokey was the name of my husband's first pet? This was important. It was a security question for a bank account.

There are many possible pitfalls and unexpected events that can happen immediately when a spouse dies. I was married to a wonderful man. We had wills and life insurance in place. I thought I was prepared, but I was not at all. Many surprises startled me and left me scurrying for solutions.

The bank put a freeze on the joint account, so I didn't have cash for a while.

Another issue was that on my husband's individual bank account, he didn't list me as a beneficiary. That account was frozen. I had to go to a probate court and did not have access to those funds for two years from the date of death.

The Social Security funds that were deposited electronically to the bank, were sent back without any notification to me. Because I did not realize the funds were not there, I was writing overdrawn checks on that account. Social Security later adjusted the amount of the electronic payment to a lower amount for just me without my spouse, and deposited it retroactively back to the time of his death.

Then the bill collectors started calling for payments for the leased car. Since my husband only had it leased in his name, I simply returned the car with a copy of the death certificate. That did not stop the harassing calls from the collectors. Do not have leased cars in both of your names unless you intend to keep the car and continue with the contract.

My husband got sick and died at home with Hospice. His failing health amassed stacks of medical bills, as it does for so many others. Sorting through them was challenging. The entities that supposedly were caring for us turned out to be financial predators. I found discrepancies. It took a lot of work, but I took the time to review each bill and pay a proper amount. In some cases, I had to negotiate a reduced payment or create a payment plan over time. I did find that the medical entities will let you negotiate. It was a very stressful time.

I have grown children who live in New York. I didn't want to burden them. They have their own lives. I didn't realize that I would need a strong support system, so I had not arranged for help. I was certainly not as prepared as I thought I was.

What I learned I learned too late.

I started talking with other widows and formed trusted confidants. I started reading the AARP newsletter. Out of pure necessity, I researched solutions online as best that I could. I had to learn to deflect the people targeting widows and widowers to take advantage in some way that I could never anticipate.

I was married to a kind, considerate, and spiritual man. Even with good communication and what we thought was a clear plan, we missed a lot of details. I know he would not have wanted me to have gone through the extra angst and stress the absence of this knowledge caused me. There are important steps we could have taken while my husband was alive that could have cleared the confusion for me later, like knowing the answers to security questions. I don't want anyone to go through the struggles that I endured. With some planning, I feel many pitfalls can be avoided. I would like to help other couples prepare for the worst by doing their best, while still together in this world. This will help their loved one make a smooth transition as the living spouse.

Minimize the Stress

You will be vulnerable after the passing of a spouse. It is unfortunate, but you will have to deal with institutional entities such as banks, credit card companies, Social Security and such. The organizations are not known for compassion, so it's best to be prepared!

Once informed of the death of your spouse, the bank will most likely put a freeze on a joint account. You may not have access to the money. Before the bank is notified, remove as much money as you can. It sounds less compassionate to be thinking of that first, but you will need the money for living until things are sorted out with your finances. Social Security checks will stop temporarily; and if it is ordinarily received electronically, the bank will send the deposits back; and this without any notification. Clearly you can understand that you will need at least three months of accessible money to pay your living expenses. This could be planned for in advance. Each of you should have a separate banking account in your name only. This is a great place to keep your "rainy day" money.

Once the Social Security departments determine how much you are now entitled to receive, it will be sent retroactively. Be sure to give them your new account number if you will not continue using the account where it was being sent.

Have a list of all recurring bank auto-payments and credit cards. Stop automatic payments on your spouse's credit card accounts for goods and services you will no longer need.

Auto leasing can be very tricky. If you or your spouse leases a car, it should only be in one name. If your spouse dies prior to the end of the lease, you can return the car without any further payment responsibilities.

Incapacitation
and the Importance of Building a Family File

According to statistics, 1.5 million Americans sustain a traumatic brain injury per year and 230,000 people are hospitalized and survive.

Six months after I married my second husband Sam, he was involved in a serious accident which rendered him comatose and resulted in traumatic brain injury. At the time that this occurred, the doctors told me that my husband would probably wind up in a vegetative state and I should prepare for his long-term care in a facility. I was devastated; however, I was positive. I arranged for the best possible hospital and rehab facility within 100 miles. We lived in upstate New York, but the best facility was an hour away in Connecticut. I fought to have him placed there. Luckily, they had room and he was transported to this wonderful facility. We were very lucky because he had, through his company, Catastrophic Insurance Coverage. He was in the hospital and rehab center over four months. I don't know how we would have afforded it had the insurance not have been in place.

The second most fortunate thing that happened was, right after we were married, we went to a lecture given by a financial advisor, and as a result, we both had a will, a living will, and each had a durable Power of Attorney. Thank God we did! When we married, I gave up my house and moved into my husband's house. My husband had children from his former marriage. His wife had died, but before that, she requested that an irrevocable trust be set up so that her children would have her half of the estate. My new husband informed me of this and I had no vision of a problem with it. It seemed fair to me. I was unaware, however, of what could have happened had I not had these legal documents in place. When I suggested to my husband's children that we both sell the assets to put him in a premier long-term health facility, I was shocked when his daughter said that this was their inheritance and she would not consider it!

Yes, I was very naive – it had never occurred to me that money meant more to these people than any loyalty or devotion to a wonderful, caring father who had gone to work every single day to feed and clothe them, put them through college, and continue with moral, ethical, and many times, financial support. Had I not had those legal documents in place, my wonderful husband would have been relegated to a state facility and I would have been removed from my home. His children planned to take over the entire estate. As Trustees to the Trust, it might have happened, but I had the Power of Attorney.

The third most fortunate event occurred when my husband recovered enough and was functional. He had residual effects, but overall, he was basically able to show marked improvement over the years. Once Sam recovered, he saw what his children had attempted to do and the utter deviousness of his progeny was very hurtful to him.

I loved my husband and whatever hurt him, hurt me. He became estranged from his kids; how terribly sad for them.

While we were close and had a good relationship, still when I asked him to share his computer information with me, I found my husband reluctant to give me all of the passwords or tell me where I could find them. He wasn't actually hiding anything. It was more a matter of his having control over his privacy. It took days of searching through his papers and computer to find information so needed after his passing to get things moving in the right direction. Some I never found.

This is not so unusual. I was not surprised to encounter widowed friends and members of my grievance group, who had no idea of how to get into their spouses' computers or phones, much less know the passwords to the programs on them.

When discussing passwords with a recalcitrant spouse, you might suggest that if something happened, and you both were incapacitated, it would be wise to have all the passwords and security questions in an alphabetized phone book. There are several online software possibilities which will store all of this. One very easy and workable software is Norton Security Vault. Then, all you need to know is the "vault" password. I was married for over 25 years and never knew that my husband's first dog's name was Smokey. Be sure to add the password book to the family file.

Circumstances might necessitate a family friend or support person to be called to "work" the computer and get all the facts and details needed. Needless to say, the book or software tool is an absolute necessity.

Speaking of the family friend or support person, the two of you should choose this person together. It might change over time. But there should always be someone in place. While you are deciding who this person should be, a choice should be made of who will preside over the service when the time comes, and who will give the eulogy. It sounds a bit untoward, but it's such a big relief to have this in place when needed … which is a personally awful time. Count on the funeral director to notify Social Security and also provide the death certificate, of which you will need at least ten.

Ultimately, the family file should contain copies of documents such as marriage certificates, any veteran's discharge or benefits, home ownership, mortgages, outstanding loans, recurring charges, and credit cards. The credit cards in a spouse's name shouldbe cancelled, as an example of use of death certificates.

Now don't forget to properly file each of your living wills, bill of sale that transfers all goods and personal possessions. You will also want to include a Health Care Surrogate document, and a Durable Power of Attorney for each spouse.

Financially, you must include trusts, most recent tax information, names of attorneys and financial advisors, checking and savings account information, and investments.

I have heard worse stories about children from former marriages than the incident with Sam and I. The single most relevant thing that saved both me and my spouse from devastating results due to his accident, were these legal documents. We went on to spend 25 happy, wonderful years together.

Yes, I was in love and trusted my husband; perhaps too much, as I never asked him to be open with me about financial situations and obligations. During his incapacity, federal and state taxes were due. I knew nothing about his tax situation. The brand-new Thunderbird had been leased and had to be returned. His financial situations before our marriage were unknown to me. He had a safe and I had no idea what the combination was. I had no idea about his investments or what recurring bills or credit cards they were responsible for paying. It all could have been so much easier for me, had I asked for, and been given, access to his private financial world.

Not Married, But Living Together? Dependents?

There are many unique situations to consider, not just blended families. I had a friend who had been a school teacher and her husband died. She later met a very nice man and they hit it off well.

She moved into his home and they lived together for 15 years. He died suddenly. They both had children from previous marriages. She got along well with his children and did not expect conflict. However, after his death, his children wanted to sell the house. My friend's name was not on the deed. She was forced to pack and move out of the house. Sadly, this also forced her to move back with her own children in another state. She lost her home. Be aware, even if you think your mate's children won't turn on you over money, think again! Forewarned is forearmed. Have legal documents ready to protect yourself.

Also, there are cases where one, or both partners, are responsible for an aging parent, a mentally challenged child or other dependent. Make preparations for these people. Know who will care for the individual(s) after your incapacitation or death. Have a caretaker or guardian in place and documented.

CHAPTER 3,
A Checklist to Complete Together as Soon as possible and Update as Often as Needed

Talk about death before it happens. As unpleasant as this topic is, it will be much more unpleasant to a surviving loved one if details are not attended to in advance. When death occurs, people are often overcome with grief and feel overwhelmed with the many decisions and details that have to be considered. Spouses can be paralyzed with indecision. Having a plan in place is critical.

If the grieving partner has a trusted person to assist with the process, that will ease the burden. Involve this support person(s) in advance by giving them copies of all pertinent documents. Plan a place in your home or nearby where this person support person(s) can assist, especially in the first few days after death.

Create a family file that should be updated every six months to a year. The number one problem in a marriage is finances. Start early. Gather your resources and note what bills need to be paid and how one person can handle the actual payments. Both partners must be aware of all of the expenses and how they will be paid, both now and after the death of a spouse. Make sure the bills can be paid and note with which fund.

This family file should have all the necessary documentation and contact information to make a smooth transition. Each partner needs to know where this file will be kept.

The family file should contain such information as listed below.

MARRIAGE CERTIFICATE
Start the file with a few certified copies of the marriage certificate.

PASSWORDS
Even if spouses have planned well, and funded adequately, the surviving spouse needs to know all the passwords, answers for security questions for passwords, PINS and other necessary data to access financial, as well as other accounts. Remember things like the garage door opener code or gate code. Not knowing passwords and codes is often the biggest issue for surviving spouses. Remember to include instructions for access to all digital assets, including social media accounts, and photos and other online cloud storage.

FINANCIAL INFORMATION

+ BUDGET
Note if paper bills are mailed and to where.
Note if electronic payments are made from bank accounts or credit cards.
Note how each bill is paid whether by paper check, online banking, credit cards, electronic payments or any other manner.
Prepare a comprehensive budget and discuss how these financial obligations will be met by the surviving spouse.

+ BANKS AND CREDIT UNIONS
Be prepared financially to have at least three months of available funds in bank accounts in each spouse's individual name to cover living expenses. Set up these

bank accounts and fund them.

For both individual and joint bank accounts, be sure that the spouse is listed as the beneficiary of each account.

If there are recurring automatic payments taken from bank accounts, note the amount and contact information for the companies being paid.

If applicable, know where the bank safety deposit box key is and have both spouses listed individually for access.

+ CREDIT CARDS

Make a list of credit cards and contact information for each card.

Note any recurring charges to these cards so they can be cancelled if no longer needed.

Each spouse should have at least one credit card in their own name.

+ BUSINESS OWNERSHIP

If a business is owned or invested in, have the related contracts in the file, and any pertinent documents.

+ INVESTMENTS

If there are stocks, bonds, and other investments, have all of that information in a known and accessible place.

+ FINANCIAL PLANNER

Perhaps you have a financial planner who can help navigate planning and keep records. Consider hiring one. Many financial planners will take even small budget clients.

+ CASH

Stash at least $2,500 cash in a secure place that offers easy access to each spouse in emergencies.

+VALUABLES

For cash, collectibles, jewelry or other valuables, know where they are kept. People frequently give cash inadvertently to charities, stuffed in clothing pockets or hidden in book pages.

+ LIFE INSURANCE

If there is a life insurance policy, have that in the file with contact information.

+ PENSION

If a pension exists, have the documents in the file. Know ahead of time if it continues for the spouse after the death of the retiree.

+ MILITARY BENEFITS

If a spouse served in the military service and there are benefits, have a copy of the discharge papers.
Note if the benefits will continue for the surviving spouse.

OTHER IMPORTANT DATA TO ORGANIZE IN YOUR FAMILY FILE

+ WILL

Have a will, a living will, and perhaps a revocable trust in place.
There are forms for simple wills online and event at office supply stores.
If your will is complex, it is wise to hire an attorney.

+ ATTORNEY

If you have one, know who your attorney is and how to contact them.
Understand in advance what fees have been pre-paid and what might be expected to be paid, and what the fees are.

+ ACCOUNTANT AND TAXES

Stay in contact with your accountant.
Have copies of the last few years of personal tax returns.
If your spouse files the tax returns, decide if the sur-

viving spouse will take on that responsibility or hire a professional.

+ PROPERTY RECORDS

If property is owned, include copies of the deeds in the file.

If there is a mortgage or lien, include those documents.

Include copies for all properties owned.

If there is a rental property, include all information, such as the renter, copy of the lease, and realtor or manager contact information if there is such a person.

If spouses are renting a residence, have a copy of the lease in the file.

Include also the policy or policies for homeowner's or renter's insurance.

+ PROPERTY AND LIVING ARRANGEMENTS

Will the surviving spouse be able to stay in the current home?

If not, perhaps plan for another person to move in to help physically and / or financially.

Moving in with a family member or another person is often the solution.

Downsizing and renting or buying a new place with lower overhead is also an option. Concerns seniors have with moving to lower-cost areas is the safety of the area and their vulnerability to crime. Talk about safety tips as a person living alone and research areas to consider well in advance. Perhaps hire a realtor so options can be researched leisurely over time.

Other solutions include senior housing options, independent living facilities, assisted living facilities, or nursing homes.

All of these choices depend on the physical needs and financial resources of the surviving spouse.

+ AUTOMOBILES

If automobiles are paid for, have the titles in the file. Have the registration and proof of insurance in the glove compartment if needed to turn in or sell the automobile, or in the event of an accident or damage.

If automobiles are in an individual's name, not jointly, the car typically can be returned and the surviving spouse will not have to pay the remaining lease payments after the spouse passes. Confirm this by reading your lease agreement.

If automobiles are being purchased, review your contract for liability for payments after death.

Have the auto insurance agent contact information available so the insurance information on an extra car or truck can be cancelled.

Are there any ongoing parking fees for the automobile? Be sure to cancel those fees when no longer needed.

Perhaps you have a car that is paid for and, in that case, have the title to the car in your file. You will need the title if you want to sell the car.

+ MEDICAL

Unless the spouse passes quickly without medical care, this can be one of the most cumbersome of all the tasks left to a widowed spouse.

Medical contacts, such as doctors, labs, and hospitals, should be readily available. Know each spouse's primary doctor especially.

Have a list of any recurring charges that should be stopped, such as medications.

Have the contact for medical insurance, and have a clear understanding of deductibles and payment obligations.

Be prepared to review any medical expenses and validate that payment is actually due for the items billed.

Ask for itemized bills.

I found articles by AARP on how to pay medical bills very informative and helpful.

+ MISCELLANEOUS EXPENSES

Little expenses add up quickly, especially when the household income declines suddenly. Remember to note recurring expenses that may no longer be needed such as subscriptions to newspapers, magazines and periodicals.

+ PERSONAL CONTACTS

Make a list of contact information, including addresses, phone numbers and email addresses. These contacts include loved ones, friends and business associates. This will make it easy to notify them for support or for updates on the spouse. These lists can also be used for birthday and holiday greetings.

+ SHARE LOVE

Most importantly, hug and say "I love you" as often as possible. It may be your last opportunity to do so.

MAKE A PLAN FOR YOUR SPOUSE, PARTNER, SIGNIFICANT OTHER

In some cases, deaths happen suddenly. Unexpected deaths are a big reason for the necessity to plan for each other in advance.

THIS BOOK

Put this book with your notes in it into the family file. Put it all in a safe place. Rest easy that you prepared yourself as best as you can.

CHAPTER 4,
Finances for the Newly Widowed

Refer to the notes and contact information you made or will make in the back of this book. Find the comprehensive family file that you made together with your spouse or partner. Contact your personal support person(s) first. You can execute your plan or have them help as needed.

Contact the Social Security office and financial institutions. If applicable, notify the life insurance company and / or military benefits office. If necessary, notify the probate office at the local county courthouse regarding your will.

These documents should have already been organized in advance and a plan should be in place to execute the changes. After death, it is time to transfer funds from the deceased's bank accounts, cancel credit cards, stop automatic delivery of medications, and other ongoing expenses. This process will go much more seamlessly with your family file completed.

CHAPTER 5,
Funeral Arrangements

The time to plan a funeral will be an emotional time and not a good time to make decisions. Have as many details as possible planned in advance. Not only does this allow for the person who has passed to participate in advance in the decision making but it also lessens the burden for the surviving spouse.

Have a plan for funeral, wake, burial or cremation. Make as many possible necessary arrangements ahead of time. Decide on casket, viewing and burial attire. Decide on a church service if appropriate. Pay in advance if possible.

Contact the funeral home. The funeral director will help to get things started by notifying the Social Security office of the death.

The funeral director will also typically place the obituary online on their website. Make a list of other publications or online sources such as church bulletins to place the obituary. Write the obituary in advance.

Also, the funeral director will get death certificates. These will be needed for all the institutions to change the status from married to widowed. The death certificate is the important first step to carrying out the changing of your documents at financial and other institutions.

CHAPTER 6
Tips for Recent Widows and Senior Concerns

Two major concerns are for day-to-day living arrangements and medical expenses.

To be better prepared to live without your partner in your residence, know how to change the batteries in the phones, the smoke detectors, remotes, computer mouse and such. Know where and how to shut off water at the main water source. Know where the electrical breaker box is and label each breaker for the appropriate area of the house. Know what a GFI outlet is and how to reset it. Know which light bulb goes in the ceiling light and how to change them. Know how to change the AC filters monthly. Whatever home maintenance necessary, such as do you have the gutters cleaned, or shutters maintained and by whom? In advance, have the names and phone numbers of home maintenance workers for future use.

Another cumbersome task can be dealing with medical bills. Have a separate credit card and bank account to pay these bills from and keep records for tax purposes. If you find you're being bombarded with medical bills, don't pay them immediately. Call the companies and say you want an itemized document with the costs mailed to you. You must check the bills to be sure they haven't been paid already. There are a lot of mistakes in the medical billing departments! You legally have 30 days after a medical bill collector calls to ask for proof that you owe the amount demanded. If you're responsible, set up a payment plan. Hopefully, all medical bills were paid in the credit card held in your spouse's name only. If your income is $25,000 or less, contact a non-profit group called RIP Medical Debt to see if you qualify for debt forgiveness.

First of all, don't make any important decisions for a year.
Be prepared and ready to understand and come to terms with inevitable senior concerns.

Senior concerns can include:

+ If you don't already have a smart phone, get one and learn how to use it. It will come in handy now that you will inevitably have more responsibility.
+ Don't try to answer all phone calls or emails. Respond to important ones only.
+ Beware of phone scams and fraudulent calls. Scammers review obituaries and know widows are vulnerable.
+ Beware of inactivity and loneliness.
+ Talk with a professional about any feelings of self-pity or guilt.
+ Physical abilities -- Get someone to lift and carry heavy objects, climb ladders, open jars, clean the pool, and do the yard work.
+ Mental waning -- Forgetfulness does not improve with age so adjust to it.
+ Write everything down and date it. Keep note pads and pens handy.
+ Stay organized -- Keep a paper calendar of doctor's appointments, social events and such.

In summary, I hope this little book has spurned you to take action to provide a smooth transition to a new and different life.

Family File Notes

Family File Notes

Family File Notes

Family File Notes

Family File Notes